To

all the very best
for your future

Lov you Lots

Mum + Dad

sept 1992.

THE HORSE

RONALD DUNCAN

with drawings by Alan Langford

SOUVENIR PRESS

This Cavalcade of Grace now stands,
it speaks in silence.

Its story is the story of this land.

Where in this wide world, can man
find nobility without pride,

friendship without envy or
beauty without vanity?

Here, where grace is laced with muscle,
and strength by gentleness confined.

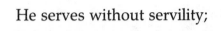

He serves without servility;

he has fought without enmity.

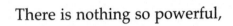There is nothing so powerful,

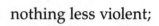

nothing less violent;

there is nothing so quick,

nothing so patient.

England's past has been borne
on his back.

All our history is his industry:

we are his heirs, he our inheritance.

Ladies and Gentlemen: THE HORSE!

First published 1990 by Souvenir Press Ltd,
43 Great Russell Street, London WC1B 3PA
and simultaneously in Canada

ISBN 0 285 63003 2

Printed and bound in Great Britain by
BPCC Hazell Books
Aylesbury, Bucks, England
Member of BPCC Ltd.